Our Humble Request:

We Love Feedback, please do consider leaving us a review! Also, we'd Love to stay in touch, please visit our website: https://www.tiesthatbindpublishing.com

If you're ever in the neighborhood, drop by and visit us on our social media!

Facebook: https://bit.ly/3slmA7N
Instagram: https://bit.ly/3dEXQ6i
Twitter: https://Twitter.com/ttbp20
YouTube: https://bit.ly/37CukdN

Have You Seen My Password(s)? Username & Password Journal

By: LaTia & William Russell

This U & P Belongs To:

_____

_____

_____

Intro:

If you're anything like us, you have an infinite number usernames and passwords, all with different requirements! Some require 6-20 letters, numbers, special character sequences (uppercase, lowercase... backwards.... HA!). Others require more or less than above without special characters or specific special characters. How can you keep up?! No, seriously, how? If I had $1 for every time, I had to.... yep, you guessed it, reset my password. Well, I would probably be writing this introduction from the beach instead of the current, snowy, frigid climate that I'm currently in. Just this past week, I must've hit my personal best in having to reset my password for various areas of my life that I need to access electronically. That got me thinking, why isn't there something nice and neat already available to help me keep up with all of this information?! Then *Ding* the lightbulb came on, create said thing, to help your fellow human (or other being depending on how you identify; we're all about inclusivity here) do just that. So, here you go, our gift to you...your U (username) & P (password) tracker. And for those of you who like control, we've given you what you need, feel free to organize your categories in whatever way works best for you (see category suggestions on the next page, or, create your own)!

You can thank us by purchasing a ton, so we can create the next thing you desperately need to make your life easier from the beach (we're kidding.... kind of)!

The rest is up to you!

Happy Tracking!

USERNAME & PASSWORD TRACKER, CATEGORIES

Email (Personal & Professional)

Social Media (i.e., FB, IG, Twitter, etc.;)

Finance (i.e., Online Banking, credit cards, etc.;)

Utilities (i.e., wi-fi, electricity, etc.;)

Education (i.e., school log-in portals, school reminder applications)

Entertainment (i.e., streaming services, etc.;)

Shopping & Food (i.e., grocery delivery, food delivery services, online shopping)

Travel (i.e., travel sites, airlines, etc.;)

Health & Fitness (i.e., medical information, patient records, fitness subscriptions, etc.)

Other (i.e., Apps)

Website:_____

Website:_____

Username:_____

Password:_____

Last 3 Passwords:_____

Important to Note (i.e. date reminder):_____

_____

》《·》《·》《·》《·》《·》《·》《·》《·》《·

Website:_____

Website:_____

Username:_____

Password:_____

Last 3 Passwords:_____

Important to Note (i.e. date reminder):_____

_____

》《·》《·》《·》《·》《·》《·》《·》《·》《·

Website:_____

Website:_____

Username:_____

Password:_____

Last 3 Passwords:_____

Important to Note (i.e. date reminder):_____

_____

_____

Website:_____

Username:_____

Password:_____

Last 3 Passwords:_____

Important to Note (i.e. date reminder):_____

_____

》《·》《·》《·》《·》《·》《·》《·》《·》《·

_____

Website:_____

Username:_____

Password:_____

Last 3 Passwords:_____

Important to Note (i.e. date reminder):_____

_____

》《·》《·》《·》《·》《·》《·》《·》《·》《·

_____

Website:_____

Username:_____

Password:_____

Last 3 Passwords:_____

Important to Note (i.e. date reminder):_____

_____

_____

Website:_____

Username:_____

Password:_____

Last 3 Passwords:_____

Important to Note (i.e. date reminder):_____

_____

》《·》《·》《·》《·》《·》《·》《·》《·》《·

_____

Website:_____

Username:_____

Password:_____

Last 3 Passwords:_____

Important to Note (i.e. date reminder):_____

_____

》《·》《·》《·》《·》《·》《·》《·》《·》《·

_____

Website:_____

Username:_____

Password:_____

Last 3 Passwords:_____

Important to Note (i.e. date reminder):_____

_____

Website:_____

Website:_____

Username:_____

Password:_____

Last 3 Passwords:_____

Important to Note (i.e. date reminder):_____

〉〈‹·〉〉〈‹·〉〉〈‹·〉〉〈‹·〉〉〈‹·〉〉〈‹·〉〉〈‹·〉〉〈‹·〉〉〈‹·〉〉〈‹·

Website:_____

Username:_____

Password:_____

Last 3 Passwords:_____

Important to Note (i.e. date reminder):_____

〉〈‹·〉〉〈‹·〉〉〈‹·〉〉〈‹·〉〉〈‹·〉〉〈‹·〉〉〈‹·〉〉〈‹·〉〉〈‹·〉〉〈‹·

Website:_____

Username:_____

Password:_____

Last 3 Passwords:_____

Important to Note (i.e. date reminder):_____

_____

Website:_____

Username:_____

Password:_____

Last 3 Passwords:_____

Important to Note (i.e. date reminder):_____

_____

_____

Website:_____

Username:_____

Password:_____

Last 3 Passwords:_____

Important to Note (i.e. date reminder):_____

_____

_____

Website:_____

Username:_____

Password:_____

Last 3 Passwords:_____

Important to Note (i.e. date reminder):_____

_____

_____

Website:_____

Username:_____

Password:_____

Last 3 Passwords:_____

Important to Note (i.e. date reminder):_____

_____

》《·》《·》《·》《·》《·》《·》《·》《·》《·

_____

Website:_____

Username:_____

Password:_____

Last 3 Passwords:_____

Important to Note (i.e. date reminder):_____

_____

》《·》《·》《·》《·》《·》《·》《·》《·》《·

_____

Website:_____

Username:_____

Password:_____

Last 3 Passwords:_____

Important to Note (i.e. date reminder):_____

_____

_____

Website:_____

Username:_____

Password:_____

Last 3 Passwords:_____

Important to Note (i.e. date reminder):_____

_____

»《·》《·》《·》《·》《·》《·》《·》《·》《·》《·

_____

Website:_____

Username:_____

Password:_____

Last 3 Passwords:_____

Important to Note (i.e. date reminder):_____

_____

»《·》《·》《·》《·》《·》《·》《·》《·》《·》《·

_____

Website:_____

Username:_____

Password:_____

Last 3 Passwords:_____

Important to Note (i.e. date reminder):_____

_____

_____

Website:_____

Username:_____

Password:_____

Last 3 Passwords:_____

Important to Note (i.e. date reminder):_____

_____

》《·》《·》《·》《·》《·》《·》《·》《·》《·》《·

_____

Website:_____

Username:_____

Password:_____

Last 3 Passwords:_____

Important to Note (i.e. date reminder):_____

_____

》《·》《·》《·》《·》《·》《·》《·》《·》《·》《·

_____

Website:_____

Username:_____

Password:_____

Last 3 Passwords:_____

Important to Note (i.e. date reminder):_____

_____

_____

Website:_____

Username:_____

Password:_____

Last 3 Passwords:_____

Important to Note (i.e. date reminder):_____

_____

》《•》《•》《•》《•》《•》《•》《•》《•》《•

_____

Website:_____

Username:_____

Password:_____

Last 3 Passwords:_____

Important to Note (i.e. date reminder):_____

_____

》《•》《•》《•》《•》《•》《•》《•》《•》《•

_____

Website:_____

Username:_____

Password:_____

Last 3 Passwords:_____

Important to Note (i.e. date reminder):_____

_____

_____

Website:_____

Username:_____

Password:_____

Last 3 Passwords:_____

Important to Note (i.e. date reminder):_____

_____

»《·》《·》《·》《·》《·》《·》《·》《·》《·》《·

_____

Website:_____

Username:_____

Password:_____

Last 3 Passwords:_____

Important to Note (i.e. date reminder):_____

_____

»《·》《·》《·》《·》《·》《·》《·》《·》《·

_____

Website:_____

Username:_____

Password:_____

Last 3 Passwords:_____

Important to Note (i.e. date reminder):_____

_____

_____

Website:_____

Username:_____

Password:_____

Last 3 Passwords:_____

Important to Note (i.e. date reminder):_____

_____

»《‹·›》《‹›》《‹·›》《‹·›》《‹·›》《‹·›》《‹·›》《‹·›》《‹·

_____

Website:_____

Username:_____

Password:_____

Last 3 Passwords:_____

Important to Note (i.e. date reminder):_____

_____

»《‹·›》《‹›》《‹·›》《‹·›》《‹·›》《‹·›》《‹·›》《‹·›》《‹·

_____

Website:_____

Username:_____

Password:_____

Last 3 Passwords:_____

Important to Note (i.e. date reminder):_____

_____

_____

Website:_____

Username:_____

Password:_____

Last 3 Passwords:_____

Important to Note (i.e. date reminder):_____

_____

》《·》《·》《·》《·》《·》《·》《·》《·》《·

_____

Website:_____

Username:_____

Password:_____

Last 3 Passwords:_____

Important to Note (i.e. date reminder):_____

_____

》《·》《·》《·》《·》《·》《·》《·》《·》《·

_____

Website:_____

Username:_____

Password:_____

Last 3 Passwords:_____

Important to Note (i.e. date reminder):_____

_____

_____

Website:_____

Username:_____

Password:_____

Last 3 Passwords:_____

Important to Note (i.e. date reminder):_____

_____

_____

Website:_____

Username:_____

Password:_____

Last 3 Passwords:_____

Important to Note (i.e. date reminder):_____

_____

_____

Website:_____

Username:_____

Password:_____

Last 3 Passwords:_____

Important to Note (i.e. date reminder):_____

_____

_____

Website:_____

Username:_____

Password:_____

Last 3 Passwords:_____

Important to Note (i.e. date reminder):_____

_____

》《·》《·》《·》《·》《·》《·》《·》《·》《·

_____

Website:_____

Username:_____

Password:_____

Last 3 Passwords:_____

Important to Note (i.e. date reminder):_____

_____

》《·》《·》《·》《·》《·》《·》《·》《·》《·

_____

Website:_____

Username:_____

Password:_____

Last 3 Passwords:_____

Important to Note (i.e. date reminder):_____

_____

_____

Website:_____

Username:_____

Password:_____

Last 3 Passwords:_____

Important to Note (i.e. date reminder):_____

_____

》《·》《·》《·》《·》《·》《·》《·》《·》《·》《·

_____

Website:_____

Username:_____

Password:_____

Last 3 Passwords:_____

Important to Note (i.e. date reminder):_____

_____

》《·》《·》《·》《·》《·》《·》《·》《·》《·》《·

_____

Website:_____

Username:_____

Password:_____

Last 3 Passwords:_____

Important to Note (i.e. date reminder):_____

_____

Website:_____

Website:_____

Username:_____

Password:_____

Last 3 Passwords:_____

Important to Note (i.e. date reminder):_____

》《‹·》《‹·》《‹·》《‹·》《‹·》《‹·》《‹·》《‹·》《‹·》《‹·

Website:_____

Username:_____

Password:_____

Last 3 Passwords:_____

Important to Note (i.e. date reminder):_____

》《‹·》《‹·》《‹·》《‹·》《‹·》《‹·》《‹·》《‹·》《‹·》《‹·

Website:_____

Username:_____

Password:_____

Last 3 Passwords:_____

Important to Note (i.e. date reminder):_____

_____

Website:_____

Username:_____

Password:_____

Last 3 Passwords:_____

Important to Note (i.e. date reminder):_____

_____

_____

Website:_____

Username:_____

Password:_____

Last 3 Passwords:_____

Important to Note (i.e. date reminder):_____

_____

_____

Website:_____

Username:_____

Password:_____

Last 3 Passwords:_____

Important to Note (i.e. date reminder):_____

_____

_____

Website:_____

Username:_____

Password:_____

Last 3 Passwords:_____

Important to Note (i.e. date reminder):_____

_____

»《·»《·»《·»《·»《·»《·»《·»《·»《·»《·

_____

Website:_____

Username:_____

Password:_____

Last 3 Passwords:_____

Important to Note (i.e. date reminder):_____

_____

»《·»《·»《·»《·»《·»《·»《·»《·»《·»《·

_____

Website:_____

Username:_____

Password:_____

Last 3 Passwords:_____

Important to Note (i.e. date reminder):_____

_____

_____

Website:_____

Username:_____

Password:_____

Last 3 Passwords:_____

Important to Note (i.e. date reminder):_____

_____

》《•》《•》《•》《•》《•》《•》《•》《•》《•》《•

_____

Website:_____

Username:_____

Password:_____

Last 3 Passwords:_____

Important to Note (i.e. date reminder):_____

_____

》《•》《•》《•》《•》《•》《•》《•》《•》《•》《•

_____

Website:_____

Username:_____

Password:_____

Last 3 Passwords:_____

Important to Note (i.e. date reminder):_____

_____

_____

Website:_____

Username:_____

Password:_____

Last 3 Passwords:_____

Important to Note (i.e. date reminder):_____

_____

》《‹•》《‹•》《‹•》《‹•》《‹•》《‹•》《‹•》《‹•》《‹•》《‹•

_____

Website:_____

Username:_____

Password:_____

Last 3 Passwords:_____

Important to Note (i.e. date reminder):_____

_____

》《‹•》《‹•》《‹•》《‹•》《‹•》《‹•》《‹•》《‹•》《‹•》《‹•

_____

Website:_____

Username:_____

Password:_____

Last 3 Passwords:_____

Important to Note (i.e. date reminder):_____

_____

Website:_____

Username:_____

Password:_____

Last 3 Passwords:_____

Important to Note (i.e. date reminder):_____

》《•》《•》《•》《•》《•》《•》《•》《•》《•

Website:_____

Username:_____

Password:_____

Last 3 Passwords:_____

Important to Note (i.e. date reminder):_____

》《•》《•》《•》《•》《•》《•》《•》《•》《•

Website:_____

Username:_____

Password:_____

Last 3 Passwords:_____

Important to Note (i.e. date reminder):_____

_____

Website:_____

Username:_____

Password:_____

Last 3 Passwords:_____

Important to Note (i.e. date reminder):_____

_____

》《•》》《•》》《•》》《•》》《•》》《•》》《•》》《•》》《•》》《•

_____

Website:_____

Username:_____

Password:_____

Last 3 Passwords:_____

Important to Note (i.e. date reminder):_____

_____

》《•》》《•》》《•》》《•》》《•》》《•》》《•》》《•》》《•》》《•

_____

Website:_____

Username:_____

Password:_____

Last 3 Passwords:_____

Important to Note (i.e. date reminder):_____

_____

_____

Website:_____

Username:_____

Password:_____

Last 3 Passwords:_____

Important to Note (i.e. date reminder):_____

_____

_____

Website:_____

Username:_____

Password:_____

Last 3 Passwords:_____

Important to Note (i.e. date reminder):_____

_____

_____

Website:_____

Username:_____

Password:_____

Last 3 Passwords:_____

Important to Note (i.e. date reminder):_____

_____

_____

Website:_____

Username:_____

Password:_____

Last 3 Passwords:_____

Important to Note (i.e. date reminder):_____

_____

»《·》《·》《·》《·》《·》《·》《·》《·》《·》《·

_____

Website:_____

Username:_____

Password:_____

Last 3 Passwords:_____

Important to Note (i.e. date reminder):_____

_____

»《·》《·》《·》《·》《·》《·》《·》《·》《·》《·

_____

Website:_____

Username:_____

Password:_____

Last 3 Passwords:_____

Important to Note (i.e. date reminder):_____

_____

_____

Website:_____

Username:_____

Password:_____

Last 3 Passwords:_____

Important to Note (i.e. date reminder):_____

_____

》《•》《•》《•》《•》《•》《•》《•》《•》《•》《•

_____

Website:_____

Username:_____

Password:_____

Last 3 Passwords:_____

Important to Note (i.e. date reminder):_____

_____

》《•》《•》《•》《•》《•》《•》《•》《•》《•》《•

_____

Website:_____

Username:_____

Password:_____

Last 3 Passwords:_____

Important to Note (i.e. date reminder):_____

_____

_____

Website:_____

Username:_____

Password:_____

Last 3 Passwords:_____

Important to Note (i.e. date reminder):_____

_____

》《·》《·》《·》《·》《·》《·》《·》《·》《·

_____

Website:_____

Username:_____

Password:_____

Last 3 Passwords:_____

Important to Note (i.e. date reminder):_____

_____

》《·》《·》《·》《·》《·》《·》《·》《·》《·

_____

Website:_____

Username:_____

Password:_____

Last 3 Passwords:_____

Important to Note (i.e. date reminder):_____

_____

_____

Website:_____

Username:_____

Password:_____

Last 3 Passwords:_____

Important to Note (i.e. date reminder):_____

_____

_____

Website:_____

Username:_____

Password:_____

Last 3 Passwords:_____

Important to Note (i.e. date reminder):_____

_____

_____

Website:_____

Username:_____

Password:_____

Last 3 Passwords:_____

Important to Note (i.e. date reminder):_____

_____

_____

Website:_____

Username:_____

Password:_____

Last 3 Passwords:_____

Important to Note (i.e. date reminder):_____

_____

》《‹·》《‹·》《‹·》《‹·》《‹·》《‹·》《‹·》《‹·》《‹·

_____

Website:_____

Username:_____

Password:_____

Last 3 Passwords:_____

Important to Note (i.e. date reminder):_____

_____

》《‹·》《‹·》《‹·》《‹·》《‹·》《‹·》《‹·》《‹·》《‹·

_____

Website:_____

Username:_____

Password:_____

Last 3 Passwords:_____

Important to Note (i.e. date reminder):_____

_____

_____

Website:_____

Username:_____

Password:_____

Last 3 Passwords:_____

Important to Note (i.e. date reminder):_____

_____

_____

Website:_____

Username:_____

Password:_____

Last 3 Passwords:_____

Important to Note (i.e. date reminder):_____

_____

_____

Website:_____

Username:_____

Password:_____

Last 3 Passwords:_____

Important to Note (i.e. date reminder):_____

_____

_____

Website:_____

Username:_____

Password:_____

Last 3 Passwords:_____

Important to Note (i.e. date reminder):_____

_____

»《·》《·》《·》《·》《·》《·》《·》《·》《·》《·

_____

Website:_____

Username:_____

Password:_____

Last 3 Passwords:_____

Important to Note (i.e. date reminder):_____

_____

»《·》《·》《·》《·》《·》《·》《·》《·》《·》《·

_____

Website:_____

Username:_____

Password:_____

Last 3 Passwords:_____

Important to Note (i.e. date reminder):_____

_____

_____

Website:_____

Username:_____

Password:_____

Last 3 Passwords:_____

Important to Note (i.e. date reminder):_____

_____

_____

Website:_____

Username:_____

Password:_____

Last 3 Passwords:_____

Important to Note (i.e. date reminder):_____

_____

_____

Website:_____

Username:_____

Password:_____

Last 3 Passwords:_____

Important to Note (i.e. date reminder):_____

_____

_____

Website:_____

Username:_____

Password:_____

Last 3 Passwords:_____

Important to Note (i.e. date reminder):_____

_____

》《•》《•》《•》《•》《•》《•》《•》《•》《•》《•

_____

Website:_____

Username:_____

Password:_____

Last 3 Passwords:_____

Important to Note (i.e. date reminder):_____

_____

》《•》《•》《•》《•》《•》《•》《•》《•》《•》《•

_____

Website:_____

Username:_____

Password:_____

Last 3 Passwords:_____

Important to Note (i.e. date reminder):_____

_____

_____

Website:_____

Username:_____

Password:_____

Last 3 Passwords:_____

Important to Note (i.e. date reminder):_____

_____

_____

Website:_____

Username:_____

Password:_____

Last 3 Passwords:_____

Important to Note (i.e. date reminder):_____

_____

_____

Website:_____

Username:_____

Password:_____

Last 3 Passwords:_____

Important to Note (i.e. date reminder):_____

_____

_____

Website:_____

Username:_____

Password:_____

Last 3 Passwords:_____

Important to Note (i.e. date reminder):_____

_____

》《·》《·》《·》《·》《·》《·》《·》《·》《·

_____

Website:_____

Username:_____

Password:_____

Last 3 Passwords:_____

Important to Note (i.e. date reminder):_____

_____

》《·》《·》《·》《·》《·》《·》《·》《·》《·

_____

Website:_____

Username:_____

Password:_____

Last 3 Passwords:_____

Important to Note (i.e. date reminder):_____

_____

_____

Website:_____

Username:_____

Password:_____

Last 3 Passwords:_____

Important to Note (i.e. date reminder):_____

_____

_____

Website:_____

Username:_____

Password:_____

Last 3 Passwords:_____

Important to Note (i.e. date reminder):_____

_____

_____

Website:_____

Username:_____

Password:_____

Last 3 Passwords:_____

Important to Note (i.e. date reminder):_____

_____

_____

Website:_____

Username:_____

Password:_____

Last 3 Passwords:_____

Important to Note (i.e. date reminder):_____

_____

》《‹·》《‹·》《‹·》《‹·》《‹·》《‹·》《‹·》《‹·》《‹·

_____

Website:_____

Username:_____

Password:_____

Last 3 Passwords:_____

Important to Note (i.e. date reminder):_____

_____

》《‹·》《‹·》《‹·》《‹·》《‹·》《‹·》《‹·》《‹·》《‹·

_____

Website:_____

Username:_____

Password:_____

Last 3 Passwords:_____

Important to Note (i.e. date reminder):_____

_____

Website:

Username:

Password:

Last 3 Passwords:

Important to Note (i.e. date reminder):

〉〉《·〉〉《·〉〉《·〉〉《·〉〉《·〉〉《·〉〉《·〉〉《·〉〉《·

Website:

Username:

Password:

Last 3 Passwords:

Important to Note (i.e. date reminder):

〉〉《·〉〉《·〉〉《·〉〉《·〉〉《·〉〉《·〉〉《·〉〉《·〉〉《·

Website:

Username:

Password:

Last 3 Passwords:

Important to Note (i.e. date reminder):

_____

Website:_____

Username:_____

Password:_____

Last 3 Passwords:_____

Important to Note (i.e. date reminder):_____

_____

》《·》《·》《·》《·》《·》《·》《·》《·》《·

_____

Website:_____

Username:_____

Password:_____

Last 3 Passwords:_____

Important to Note (i.e. date reminder):_____

_____

》《·》《·》《·》《·》《·》《·》《·》《·》《·

_____

Website:_____

Username:_____

Password:_____

Last 3 Passwords:_____

Important to Note (i.e. date reminder):_____

_____

_____

Website:_____

Username:_____

Password:_____

Last 3 Passwords:_____

Important to Note (i.e. date reminder):_____

_____

_____

Website:_____

Username:_____

Password:_____

Last 3 Passwords:_____

Important to Note (i.e. date reminder):_____

_____

_____

Website:_____

Username:_____

Password:_____

Last 3 Passwords:_____

Important to Note (i.e. date reminder):_____

_____

_____

Website:_____

Username:_____

Password:_____

Last 3 Passwords:_____

Important to Note (i.e. date reminder):_____

_____

》《·》《·》《·》《·》《·》《·》《·》《·》《·》《·

_____

Website:_____

Username:_____

Password:_____

Last 3 Passwords:_____

Important to Note (i.e. date reminder):_____

_____

》《·》《·》《·》《·》《·》《·》《·》《·》《·》《·

_____

Website:_____

Username:_____

Password:_____

Last 3 Passwords:_____

Important to Note (i.e. date reminder):_____

_____

_____

Website:_____

Username:_____

Password:_____

Last 3 Passwords:_____

Important to Note (i.e. date reminder):_____

_____

_____

Website:_____

Username:_____

Password:_____

Last 3 Passwords:_____

Important to Note (i.e. date reminder):_____

_____

_____

Website:_____

Username:_____

Password:_____

Last 3 Passwords:_____

Important to Note (i.e. date reminder):_____

_____

_____

Website:_____

Username:_____

Password:_____

Last 3 Passwords:_____

Important to Note (i.e. date reminder):_____

_____

》《•》《•》《•》《•》《•》《•》《•》《•》《•》《•

_____

Website:_____

Username:_____

Password:_____

Last 3 Passwords:_____

Important to Note (i.e. date reminder):_____

_____

》《•》《•》《•》《•》《•》《•》《•》《•》《•》《•

_____

Website:_____

Username:_____

Password:_____

Last 3 Passwords:_____

Important to Note (i.e. date reminder):_____

_____

_____

Website:_____

Username:_____

Password:_____

Last 3 Passwords:_____

Important to Note (i.e. date reminder):_____

_____

>><<·>><<·>><<·>><<·>><<·>><<·>><<·>><<·>><<·>><<·

_____

Website:_____

Username:_____

Password:_____

Last 3 Passwords:_____

Important to Note (i.e. date reminder):_____

_____

>><<·>><<·>><<·>><<·>><<·>><<·>><<·>><<·>><<·>><<·

_____

Website:_____

Username:_____

Password:_____

Last 3 Passwords:_____

Important to Note (i.e. date reminder):_____

_____

_____

_____

_ne:_____

_assword:_____

Last 3 Passwords:_____

Important to Note (i.e. date reminder):_____

_____

》《·》《·》《·》《·》《·》《·》《·》《·》《·

_____

Website:_____

Username:_____

Password:_____

Last 3 Passwords:_____

Important to Note (i.e. date reminder):_____

_____

》《·》《·》《·》《·》《·》《·》《·》《·》《·

_____

Website:_____

Username:_____

Password:_____

Last 3 Passwords:_____

Important to Note (i.e. date reminder):_____

_____

_____

Website:_____

Username:_____

Password:_____

Last 3 Passwords:_____

Important to Note (i.e. date reminder):_____

_____

_____

Website:_____

Username:_____

Password:_____

Last 3 Passwords:_____

Important to Note (i.e. date reminder):_____

_____

_____

Website:_____

Username:_____

Password:_____

Last 3 Passwords:_____

Important to Note (i.e. date reminder):_____

_____

_____

Website:_____

Username:_____

Password:_____

Last 3 Passwords:_____

Important to Note (i.e. date reminder):_____

_____

_____

Website:_____

Username:_____

Password:_____

Last 3 Passwords:_____

Important to Note (i.e. date reminder):_____

_____

_____

Website:_____

Username:_____

Password:_____

Last 3 Passwords:_____

Important to Note (i.e. date reminder):_____

_____

_____

Website:_____

Username:_____

Password:_____

Last 3 Passwords:_____

Important to Note (i.e. date reminder):_____

_____

_____

Website:_____

Username:_____

Password:_____

Last 3 Passwords:_____

Important to Note (i.e. date reminder):_____

_____

_____

Website:_____

Username:_____

Password:_____

Last 3 Passwords:_____

Important to Note (i.e. date reminder):_____

_____

_____

Website:_____

Username:_____

Password:_____

Last 3 Passwords:_____

Important to Note (i.e. date reminder):_____

_____

》《·》《·》《·》《·》《·》《·》《·》《·》《·》《·

_____

Website:_____

Username:_____

Password:_____

Last 3 Passwords:_____

Important to Note (i.e. date reminder):_____

_____

》《·》《·》《·》《·》《·》《·》《·》《·》《·》《·

_____

Website:_____

Username:_____

Password:_____

Last 3 Passwords:_____

Important to Note (i.e. date reminder):_____

_____

Website:_____

Username:_____

Password:_____

Last 3 Passwords:_____

Important to Note (i.e. date reminder):_____

Website:_____

Username:_____

Password:_____

Last 3 Passwords:_____

Important to Note (i.e. date reminder):_____

Website:_____

Username:_____

Password:_____

Last 3 Passwords:_____

Important to Note (i.e. date reminder):_____

_____

Website:_____

Username:_____

Password:_____

Last 3 Passwords:_____

Important to Note (i.e. date reminder):_____

_____

》《·》《·》《·》《·》《·》《·》《·》《·》《·

_____

Website:_____

Username:_____

Password:_____

Last 3 Passwords:_____

Important to Note (i.e. date reminder):_____

_____

》《·》《·》《·》《·》《·》《·》《·》《·》《·

_____

Website:_____

Username:_____

Password:_____

Last 3 Passwords:_____

Important to Note (i.e. date reminder):_____

_____

_____

Website:_____

Username:_____

Password:_____

Last 3 Passwords:_____

Important to Note (i.e. date reminder):_____

_____

_____

Website:_____

Username:_____

Password:_____

Last 3 Passwords:_____

Important to Note (i.e. date reminder):_____

_____

_____

Website:_____

Username:_____

Password:_____

Last 3 Passwords:_____

Important to Note (i.e. date reminder):_____

_____

_____

Website:_____

Username:_____

Password:_____

Last 3 Passwords:_____

Important to Note (i.e. date reminder):_____

_____

»《‹·›»《‹·›»《‹·›»《‹·›»《‹·›»《‹·›»《‹·›»《‹·›»《·

_____

Website:_____

Username:_____

Password:_____

Last 3 Passwords:_____

Important to Note (i.e. date reminder):_____

_____

»《‹·›»《‹·›»《‹·›»《‹·›»《‹·›»《‹·›»《‹·›»《‹·›»《·

_____

Website:_____

Username:_____

Password:_____

Last 3 Passwords:_____

Important to Note (i.e. date reminder):_____

_____

_____

Website:_____

Username:_____

Password:_____

Last 3 Passwords:_____

Important to Note (i.e. date reminder):_____

_____

_____

Website:_____

Username:_____

Password:_____

Last 3 Passwords:_____

Important to Note (i.e. date reminder):_____

_____

_____

Website:_____

Username:_____

Password:_____

Last 3 Passwords:_____

Important to Note (i.e. date reminder):_____

_____

_____

Website:_____

Username:_____

Password:_____

Last 3 Passwords:_____

Important to Note (i.e. date reminder):_____

_____

》《·》《·》《·》《·》《·》《·》《·》《·》《·》《·

_____

Website:_____

Username:_____

Password:_____

Last 3 Passwords:_____

Important to Note (i.e. date reminder):_____

_____

》《·》《·》《·》《·》《·》《·》《·》《·》《·》《·

_____

Website:_____

Username:_____

Password:_____

Last 3 Passwords:_____

Important to Note (i.e. date reminder):_____

_____

_____

Website:_____

Username:_____

Password:_____

Last 3 Passwords:_____

Important to Note (i.e. date reminder):_____

_____

》《‹·》《‹·》《‹·》《‹·》《‹·》《‹·》《‹·》《‹·》《‹·

_____

Website:_____

Username:_____

Password:_____

Last 3 Passwords:_____

Important to Note (i.e. date reminder):_____

_____

》《‹·》《‹·》《‹·》《‹·》《‹·》《‹·》《‹·》《‹·》《‹·

_____

Website:_____

Username:_____

Password:_____

Last 3 Passwords:_____

Important to Note (i.e. date reminder):_____

_____

_____

Website:_____

Username:_____

Password:_____

Last 3 Passwords:_____

Important to Note (i.e. date reminder):_____

_____

»《‹·›》《‹·›》《‹·›》《‹·›》《‹·›》《‹·›》《‹·›》《‹·›》《‹·

_____

Website:_____

Username:_____

Password:_____

Last 3 Passwords:_____

Important to Note (i.e. date reminder):_____

_____

»《‹·›》《‹·›》《‹·›》《‹·›》《‹·›》《‹·›》《‹·›》《‹·›》《‹·

_____

Website:_____

Username:_____

Password:_____

Last 3 Passwords:_____

Important to Note (i.e. date reminder):_____

_____

_____

Website:_____

Username:_____

Password:_____

Last 3 Passwords:_____

Important to Note (i.e. date reminder):_____

_____

»《·»《·»《·»《·»《·»《·»《·»《·»《·»《·

_____

Website:_____

Username:_____

Password:_____

Last 3 Passwords:_____

Important to Note (i.e. date reminder):_____

_____

»《·»《·»《·»《·»《·»《·»《·»《·»《·»《·

_____

Website:_____

Username:_____

Password:_____

Last 3 Passwords:_____

Important to Note (i.e. date reminder):_____

_____

_____

Website:_____

Username:_____

Password:_____

Last 3 Passwords:_____

Important to Note (i.e. date reminder):_____

_____

》《•》《•》《•》《•》《•》《•》《•》《•》《•》《•

_____

Website:_____

Username:_____

Password:_____

Last 3 Passwords:_____

Important to Note (i.e. date reminder):_____

_____

》《•》《•》《•》《•》《•》《•》《•》《•》《•》《•

_____

Website:_____

Username:_____

Password:_____

Last 3 Passwords:_____

Important to Note (i.e. date reminder):_____

_____

_____

Website:_____

Username:_____

Password:_____

Last 3 Passwords:_____

Important to Note (i.e. date reminder):_____

_____

》《·》《·》《·》《·》《·》《·》《·》《·》《·

_____

Website:_____

Username:_____

Password:_____

Last 3 Passwords:_____

Important to Note (i.e. date reminder):_____

_____

》《·》《·》《·》《·》《·》《·》《·》《·》《·

_____

Website:_____

Username:_____

Password:_____

Last 3 Passwords:_____

Important to Note (i.e. date reminder):_____

_____

_____

Website:_____

Username:_____

Password:_____

Last 3 Passwords:_____

Important to Note (i.e. date reminder):_____

_____

》《·》《·》《·》《·》《·》《·》《·》《·》《·

_____

Website:_____

Username:_____

Password:_____

Last 3 Passwords:_____

Important to Note (i.e. date reminder):_____

_____

》《·》《·》《·》《·》《·》《·》《·》《·》《·

_____

Website:_____

Username:_____

Password:_____

Last 3 Passwords:_____

Important to Note (i.e. date reminder):_____

_____

_____

Website:_____

Username:_____

Password:_____

Last 3 Passwords:_____

Important to Note (i.e. date reminder):_____

_____

»《·»《·»《·»《·»《·»《·»《·»《·»《·»《·

_____

Website:_____

Username:_____

Password:_____

Last 3 Passwords:_____

Important to Note (i.e. date reminder):_____

_____

»《·»《·»《·»《·»《·»《·»《·»《·»《·»《·

_____

Website:_____

Username:_____

Password:_____

Last 3 Passwords:_____

Important to Note (i.e. date reminder):_____

_____

_____

Website:_____

Username:_____

Password:_____

Last 3 Passwords:_____

Important to Note (i.e. date reminder):_____

_____

»《·》《·》《·》《·》《·》《·》《·》《·》《·》《·

_____

Website:_____

Username:_____

Password:_____

Last 3 Passwords:_____

Important to Note (i.e. date reminder):_____

_____

»《·》《·》《·》《·》《·》《·》《·》《·》《·》《·

_____

Website:_____

Username:_____

Password:_____

Last 3 Passwords:_____

Important to Note (i.e. date reminder):_____

_____

_____

Website:_____

Username:_____

Password:_____

Last 3 Passwords:_____

Important to Note (i.e. date reminder):_____

_____

》《·》《·》《·》《·》《·》《·》《·》《·》《·

_____

Website:_____

Username:_____

Password:_____

Last 3 Passwords:_____

Important to Note (i.e. date reminder):_____

_____

》《·》《·》《·》《·》《·》《·》《·》《·》《·

_____

Website:_____

Username:_____

Password:_____

Last 3 Passwords:_____

Important to Note (i.e. date reminder):_____

_____

_____

Website:_____

Username:_____

Password:_____

Last 3 Passwords:_____

Important to Note (i.e. date reminder):_____

_____

》《·》《·》《·》《·》《·》《·》《·》《·》《·

_____

Website:_____

Username:_____

Password:_____

Last 3 Passwords:_____

Important to Note (i.e. date reminder):_____

_____

》《·》《·》《·》《·》《·》《·》《·》《·》《·

_____

Website:_____

Username:_____

Password:_____

Last 3 Passwords:_____

Important to Note (i.e. date reminder):_____

_____

_____

Website:_____

Username:_____

Password:_____

Last 3 Passwords:_____

Important to Note (i.e. date reminder):_____

_____

》《•》《•》《•》《•》《•》《•》《•》《•》《•》《•

_____

Website:_____

Username:_____

Password:_____

Last 3 Passwords:_____

Important to Note (i.e. date reminder):_____

_____

》《•》《•》《•》《•》《•》《•》《•》《•》《•》《•

_____

Website:_____

Username:_____

Password:_____

Last 3 Passwords:_____

Important to Note (i.e. date reminder):_____

_____

_____

Website:_____

Username:_____

Password:_____

Last 3 Passwords:_____

Important to Note (i.e. date reminder):_____

_____

»《‹·›》《‹·›》《‹·›》《‹·›》《‹·›》《‹·›》《‹·›》《‹·›》《‹·

_____

Website:_____

Username:_____

Password:_____

Last 3 Passwords:_____

Important to Note (i.e. date reminder):_____

_____

»《‹·›》《‹·›》《‹·›》《‹·›》《‹·›》《‹·›》《‹·›》《‹·›》《‹·

_____

Website:_____

Username:_____

Password:_____

Last 3 Passwords:_____

Important to Note (i.e. date reminder):_____

_____

_____

Website:_____

Username:_____

Password:_____

Last 3 Passwords:_____

Important to Note (i.e. date reminder):_____

_____

》《·》《·》《·》《·》《·》《·》《·》《·》《·》《·

_____

Website:_____

Username:_____

Password:_____

Last 3 Passwords:_____

Important to Note (i.e. date reminder):_____

_____

》《·》《·》《·》《·》《·》《·》《·》《·》《·》《·

_____

Website:_____

Username:_____

Password:_____

Last 3 Passwords:_____

Important to Note (i.e. date reminder):_____

_____

_____

Website:_____

Username:_____

Password:_____

Last 3 Passwords:_____

Important to Note (i.e. date reminder):_____

_____

»«·»«·»«·»«·»«·»«·»«·»«·»«·»«·»«·

_____

Website:_____

Username:_____

Password:_____

Last 3 Passwords:_____

Important to Note (i.e. date reminder):_____

_____

»«·»«·»«·»«·»«·»«·»«·»«·»«·»«·

_____

Website:_____

Username:_____

Password:_____

Last 3 Passwords:_____

Important to Note (i.e. date reminder):_____

_____

_____

Website:_____

Username:_____

Password:_____

Last 3 Passwords:_____

Important to Note (i.e. date reminder):_____

_____

》《·》《·》《·》《·》《·》《·》《·》《·》《·》《·

_____

Website:_____

Username:_____

Password:_____

Last 3 Passwords:_____

Important to Note (i.e. date reminder):_____

_____

》《·》《·》《·》《·》《·》《·》《·》《·》《·》《·

_____

Website:_____

Username:_____

Password:_____

Last 3 Passwords:_____

Important to Note (i.e. date reminder):_____

_____

_____

Website:_____

Username:_____

Password:_____

Last 3 Passwords:_____

Important to Note (i.e. date reminder):_____

_____

》《•》《•》《•》《•》《•》《•》《•》《•》《•》《•

_____

Website:_____

Username:_____

Password:_____

Last 3 Passwords:_____

Important to Note (i.e. date reminder):_____

_____

》《•》《•》《•》《•》《•》《•》《•》《•》《•》《•

_____

Website:_____

Username:_____

Password:_____

Last 3 Passwords:_____

Important to Note (i.e. date reminder):_____

_____

_____

Website:_____

Username:_____

Password:_____

Last 3 Passwords:_____

Important to Note (i.e. date reminder):_____

_____

》《‹·》《‹·》《‹·》《‹·》《‹·》《‹·》《‹·》《‹·》《‹·

_____

Website:_____

Username:_____

Password:_____

Last 3 Passwords:_____

Important to Note (i.e. date reminder):_____

_____

》《‹·》《‹·》《‹·》《‹·》《‹·》《‹·》《‹·》《‹·》《‹·

_____

Website:_____

Username:_____

Password:_____

Last 3 Passwords:_____

Important to Note (i.e. date reminder):_____

_____

_____

Website:_____

Username:_____

Password:_____

Last 3 Passwords:_____

Important to Note (i.e. date reminder):_____

_____

»《•》《•》《•》《•》《•》《•》《•》《•》《•》《•

_____

Website:_____

Username:_____

Password:_____

Last 3 Passwords:_____

Important to Note (i.e. date reminder):_____

_____

»《•》《•》《•》《•》《•》《•》《•》《•》《•

_____

Website:_____

Username:_____

Password:_____

Last 3 Passwords:_____

Important to Note (i.e. date reminder):_____

_____

_____

Website:_____

Username:_____

Password:_____

Last 3 Passwords:_____

Important to Note (i.e. date reminder):_____

_____

》《·》《·》《·》《·》《·》《·》《·》《·》《·》《·

_____

Website:_____

Username:_____

Password:_____

Last 3 Passwords:_____

Important to Note (i.e. date reminder):_____

_____

》《·》《·》《·》《·》《·》《·》《·》《·》《·》《·

_____

Website:_____

Username:_____

Password:_____

Last 3 Passwords:_____

Important to Note (i.e. date reminder):_____

_____

_____

Website:_____

Username:_____

Password:_____

Last 3 Passwords:_____

Important to Note (i.e. date reminder):_____

_____

»《·》《·》《·》《·》《·》《·》《·》《·》《·

_____

Website:_____

Username:_____

Password:_____

Last 3 Passwords:_____

Important to Note (i.e. date reminder):_____

_____

»《·》《·》《·》《·》《·》《·》《·》《·》《·

_____

Website:_____

Username:_____

Password:_____

Last 3 Passwords:_____

Important to Note (i.e. date reminder):_____

_____

_____

Website:_____

Username:_____

Password:_____

Last 3 Passwords:_____

Important to Note (i.e. date reminder):_____

_____

》《·》《·》《·》《·》《·》《·》《·》《·》《·

_____

Website:_____

Username:_____

Password:_____

Last 3 Passwords:_____

Important to Note (i.e. date reminder):_____

_____

》《·》《·》《·》《·》《·》《·》《·》《·》《·

_____

Website:_____

Username:_____

Password:_____

Last 3 Passwords:_____

Important to Note (i.e. date reminder):_____

_____

_____

Website:_____

Username:_____

Password:_____

Last 3 Passwords:_____

Important to Note (i.e. date reminder):_____

_____

》《·》《·》《·》《·》《·》《·》《·》《·》《·

_____

Website:_____

Username:_____

Password:_____

Last 3 Passwords:_____

Important to Note (i.e. date reminder):_____

_____

》《·》《·》《·》《·》《·》《·》《·》《·》《·

_____

Website:_____

Username:_____

Password:_____

Last 3 Passwords:_____

Important to Note (i.e. date reminder):_____

_____

_____

Website:_____

Username:_____

Password:_____

Last 3 Passwords:_____

Important to Note (i.e. date reminder):_____

_____

》《‹·》《‹·》《‹·》《‹·》《‹·》《‹·》《‹·》《‹·》《‹·》《‹·

_____

Website:_____

Username:_____

Password:_____

Last 3 Passwords:_____

Important to Note (i.e. date reminder):_____

_____

》《‹·》《‹·》《‹·》《‹·》《‹·》《‹·》《‹·》《‹·》《‹·》《‹·

_____

Website:_____

Username:_____

Password:_____

Last 3 Passwords:_____

Important to Note (i.e. date reminder):_____

_____

_____

Website:_____

Username:_____

Password:_____

Last 3 Passwords:_____

Important to Note (i.e. date reminder):_____

_____

»《·》《·》《·》《·》《·》《·》《·》《·》《·》《·

_____

Website:_____

Username:_____

Password:_____

Last 3 Passwords:_____

Important to Note (i.e. date reminder):_____

_____

»《·》《·》《·》《·》《·》《·》《·》《·》《·》《·

_____

Website:_____

Username:_____

Password:_____

Last 3 Passwords:_____

Important to Note (i.e. date reminder):_____

_____

_____

Website:_____

Username:_____

Password:_____

Last 3 Passwords:_____

Important to Note (i.e. date reminder):_____

_____

》《•》《•》《•》《•》《•》《•》《•》《•》《•

_____

Website:_____

Username:_____

Password:_____

Last 3 Passwords:_____

Important to Note (i.e. date reminder):_____

_____

》《•》《•》《•》《•》《•》《•》《•》《•》《•

_____

Website:_____

Username:_____

Password:_____

Last 3 Passwords:_____

Important to Note (i.e. date reminder):_____

_____

_____

Website:_____

Username:_____

Password:_____

Last 3 Passwords:_____

Important to Note (i.e. date reminder):_____

_____

》《·》《·》《·》《·》《·》《·》《·》《·》《·》《·

_____

Website:_____

Username:_____

Password:_____

Last 3 Passwords:_____

Important to Note (i.e. date reminder):_____

_____

》《·》《·》《·》《·》《·》《·》《·》《·》《·》《·

_____

Website:_____

Username:_____

Password:_____

Last 3 Passwords:_____

Important to Note (i.e. date reminder):_____

_____

_____

Website:_____

Username:_____

Password:_____

Last 3 Passwords:_____

Important to Note (i.e. date reminder):_____

_____

》《·》《·》《·》《·》《·》《·》《·》《·》《·

_____

Website:_____

Username:_____

Password:_____

Last 3 Passwords:_____

Important to Note (i.e. date reminder):_____

_____

》《·》《·》《·》《·》《·》《·》《·》《·》《·

_____

Website:_____

Username:_____

Password:_____

Last 3 Passwords:_____

Important to Note (i.e. date reminder):_____

_____

_____

Website:_____

Username:_____

Password:_____

Last 3 Passwords:_____

Important to Note (i.e. date reminder):_____

_____

》《•》《•》《•》《•》《•》《•》《•》《•》《•》《•

_____

Website:_____

Username:_____

Password:_____

Last 3 Passwords:_____

Important to Note (i.e. date reminder):_____

_____

》《•》《•》《•》《•》《•》《•》《•》《•》《•》《•

_____

Website:_____

Username:_____

Password:_____

Last 3 Passwords:_____

Important to Note (i.e. date reminder):_____

_____

_____

Website:_____

Username:_____

Password:_____

Last 3 Passwords:_____

Important to Note (i.e. date reminder):_____

_____

》《·》《·》《·》《·》《·》《·》《·》《·》《·》《·

_____

Website:_____

Username:_____

Password:_____

Last 3 Passwords:_____

Important to Note (i.e. date reminder):_____

_____

》《·》《·》《·》《·》《·》《·》《·》《·》《·》《·

_____

Website:_____

Username:_____

Password:_____

Last 3 Passwords:_____

Important to Note (i.e. date reminder):_____

_____

_____

Website:_____

Username:_____

Password:_____

Last 3 Passwords:_____

Important to Note (i.e. date reminder):_____

_____

»«·»«·»«·»«·»«·»«·»«·»«·»«·

_____

Website:_____

Username:_____

Password:_____

Last 3 Passwords:_____

Important to Note (i.e. date reminder):_____

_____

»«·»«·»«·»«·»«·»«·»«·»«·»«·

_____

Website:_____

Username:_____

Password:_____

Last 3 Passwords:_____

Important to Note (i.e. date reminder):_____

_____

_____

Website:_____

Username:_____

Password:_____

Last 3 Passwords:_____

Important to Note (i.e. date reminder):_____

_____

》《·》《·》《·》《·》《·》《·》《·》《·》《·》《·

_____

Website:_____

Username:_____

Password:_____

Last 3 Passwords:_____

Important to Note (i.e. date reminder):_____

_____

》《·》《·》《·》《·》《·》《·》《·》《·》《·》《·

_____

Website:_____

Username:_____

Password:_____

Last 3 Passwords:_____

Important to Note (i.e. date reminder):_____

_____

_____

Website:_____

Username:_____

Password:_____

Last 3 Passwords:_____

Important to Note (i.e. date reminder):_____

_____

»《·》《·》《·》《·》《·》《·》《·》《·》《·》《·

_____

Website:_____

Username:_____

Password:_____

Last 3 Passwords:_____

Important to Note (i.e. date reminder):_____

_____

»《·》《·》《·》《·》《·》《·》《·》《·》《·》《·

_____

Website:_____

Username:_____

Password:_____

Last 3 Passwords:_____

Important to Note (i.e. date reminder):_____

_____

_____

Website:_____

Username:_____

Password:_____

Last 3 Passwords:_____

Important to Note (i.e. date reminder):_____

_____

》《·》《·》《·》《·》《·》《·》《·》《·》《·

_____

Website:_____

Username:_____

Password:_____

Last 3 Passwords:_____

Important to Note (i.e. date reminder):_____

_____

》《·》《·》《·》《·》《·》《·》《·》《·》《·

_____

Website:_____

Username:_____

Password:_____

Last 3 Passwords:_____

Important to Note (i.e. date reminder):_____

_____

_____

Website:_____

Username:_____

Password:_____

Last 3 Passwords:_____

Important to Note (i.e. date reminder):_____

_____

»《·》《·》《·》《·》《·》《·》《·》《·》《·

_____

Website:_____

Username:_____

Password:_____

Last 3 Passwords:_____

Important to Note (i.e. date reminder):_____

_____

»《·》《·》《·》《·》《·》《·》《·》《·》《·

_____

Website:_____

Username:_____

Password:_____

Last 3 Passwords:_____

Important to Note (i.e. date reminder):_____

_____

_____

Website:_____

Username:_____

Password:_____

Last 3 Passwords:_____

Important to Note (i.e. date reminder):_____

_____

》《·》《·》《·》《·》《·》《·》《·》《·》《·》《·

_____

Website:_____

Username:_____

Password:_____

Last 3 Passwords:_____

Important to Note (i.e. date reminder):_____

_____

》《·》《·》《·》《·》《·》《·》《·》《·》《·》《·

_____

Website:_____

Username:_____

Password:_____

Last 3 Passwords:_____

Important to Note (i.e. date reminder):_____

_____

_____

Website:_____

Username:_____

Password:_____

Last 3 Passwords:_____

Important to Note (i.e. date reminder):_____

_____

》《·》《·》《·》《·》《·》《·》《·》《·》《·

_____

Website:_____

Username:_____

Password:_____

Last 3 Passwords:_____

Important to Note (i.e. date reminder):_____

_____

》《·》《·》《·》《·》《·》《·》《·》《·》《·

_____

Website:_____

Username:_____

Password:_____

Last 3 Passwords:_____

Important to Note (i.e. date reminder):_____

_____

_____

Website:_____

Username:_____

Password:_____

Last 3 Passwords:_____

Important to Note (i.e. date reminder):_____

_____

〉〈·〉〈·〉〈·〉〈·〉〈·〉〈·〉〈·〉〈·〉〈·〉〈·〉〈·

_____

Website:_____

Username:_____

Password:_____

Last 3 Passwords:_____

Important to Note (i.e. date reminder):_____

_____

〉〈·〉〈·〉〈·〉〈·〉〈·〉〈·〉〈·〉〈·〉〈·〉〈·〉〈·

_____

Website:_____

Username:_____

Password:_____

Last 3 Passwords:_____

Important to Note (i.e. date reminder):_____

_____

_____

Website:_____

Username:_____

Password:_____

Last 3 Passwords:_____

Important to Note (i.e. date reminder):_____

_____

》《·》《·》《·》《·》《·》《·》《·》《·》《·》《·

_____

Website:_____

Username:_____

Password:_____

Last 3 Passwords:_____

Important to Note (i.e. date reminder):_____

_____

》《·》《·》《·》《·》《·》《·》《·》《·》《·》《·

_____

Website:_____

Username:_____

Password:_____

Last 3 Passwords:_____

Important to Note (i.e. date reminder):_____

_____

_____

Website:_____

Username:_____

Password:_____

Last 3 Passwords:_____

Important to Note (i.e. date reminder):_____

_____

»«·»«·»«·»«·»«·»«·»«·»«·»«·»«·

_____

Website:_____

Username:_____

Password:_____

Last 3 Passwords:_____

Important to Note (i.e. date reminder):_____

_____

»«·»«·»«·»«·»«·»«·»«·»«·»«·»«·

_____

Website:_____

Username:_____

Password:_____

Last 3 Passwords:_____

Important to Note (i.e. date reminder):_____

_____

_____

Website:_____

Username:_____

Password:_____

Last 3 Passwords:_____

Important to Note (i.e. date reminder):_____

_____

》《·》《·》《·》《·》《·》《·》《·》《·》《·

_____

Website:_____

Username:_____

Password:_____

Last 3 Passwords:_____

Important to Note (i.e. date reminder):_____

_____

》《·》《·》《·》《·》《·》《·》《·》《·》《·

_____

Website:_____

Username:_____

Password:_____

Last 3 Passwords:_____

Important to Note (i.e. date reminder):_____

_____

_____

Website:_____

Username:_____

Password:_____

Last 3 Passwords:_____

Important to Note (i.e. date reminder):_____

_____

》《·》《·》《·》《·》《·》《·》《·》《·》《·

_____

Website:_____

Username:_____

Password:_____

Last 3 Passwords:_____

Important to Note (i.e. date reminder):_____

_____

》《·》《·》《·》《·》《·》《·》《·》《·》《·

_____

Website:_____

Username:_____

Password:_____

Last 3 Passwords:_____

Important to Note (i.e. date reminder):_____

_____

_____

Website:_____

Username:_____

Password:_____

Last 3 Passwords:_____

Important to Note (i.e. date reminder):_____

_____

》《·》《·》《·》《·》《·》《·》《·》《·》《·

_____

Website:_____

Username:_____

Password:_____

Last 3 Passwords:_____

Important to Note (i.e. date reminder):_____

_____

》《·》《·》《·》《·》《·》《·》《·》《·》《·

_____

Website:_____

Username:_____

Password:_____

Last 3 Passwords:_____

Important to Note (i.e. date reminder):_____

_____

_____

Website:_____

Username:_____

Password:_____

Last 3 Passwords:_____

Important to Note (i.e. date reminder):_____

_____

>)((·)>)((·)>)((·)>)((·)>)((·)>)((·)>)((·)>)((·)>)((·)>)((·

_____

Website:_____

Username:_____

Password:_____

Last 3 Passwords:_____

Important to Note (i.e. date reminder):_____

_____

>)((·)>)((·)>)((·)>)((·)>)((·)>)((·)>)((·)>)((·)>)((·)>)((·

_____

Website:_____

Username:_____

Password:_____

Last 3 Passwords:_____

Important to Note (i.e. date reminder):_____

_____

_____

Website:_____

Username:_____

Password:_____

Last 3 Passwords:_____

Important to Note (i.e. date reminder):_____

_____

》《‹·›》《‹·›》《‹·›》《‹·›》《‹·›》《‹·›》《‹·›》《‹·›》《‹·

_____

Website:_____

Username:_____

Password:_____

Last 3 Passwords:_____

Important to Note (i.e. date reminder):_____

_____

》《‹·›》《‹·›》《‹·›》《‹·›》《‹·›》《‹·›》《‹·›》《‹·›》《‹·

_____

Website:_____

Username:_____

Password:_____

Last 3 Passwords:_____

Important to Note (i.e. date reminder):_____

_____

_____

Website:_____

Username:_____

Password:_____

Last 3 Passwords:_____

Important to Note (i.e. date reminder):_____

_____

》《·》《·》《·》《·》《·》《·》《·》《·》《·

_____

Website:_____

Username:_____

Password:_____

Last 3 Passwords:_____

Important to Note (i.e. date reminder):_____

_____

》《·》《·》《·》《·》《·》《·》《·》《·》《·

_____

Website:_____

Username:_____

Password:_____

Last 3 Passwords:_____

Important to Note (i.e. date reminder):_____

_____

_____

Website:_____

Username:_____

Password:_____

Last 3 Passwords:_____

Important to Note (i.e. date reminder):_____

_____

》《·》《·》《·》《·》《·》《·》《·》《·》《·

_____

Website:_____

Username:_____

Password:_____

Last 3 Passwords:_____

Important to Note (i.e. date reminder):_____

_____

》《·》《·》《·》《·》《·》《·》《·》《·》《·

_____

Website:_____

Username:_____

Password:_____

Last 3 Passwords:_____

Important to Note (i.e. date reminder):_____

_____

_____

Website:_____

Username:_____

Password:_____

Last 3 Passwords:_____

Important to Note (i.e. date reminder):_____

_____

»《·》《·》《·》《·》《·》《·》《·》《·》《·》《·

_____

Website:_____

Username:_____

Password:_____

Last 3 Passwords:_____

Important to Note (i.e. date reminder):_____

_____

»《·》《·》《·》《·》《·》《·》《·》《·》《·》《·

_____

Website:_____

Username:_____

Password:_____

Last 3 Passwords:_____

Important to Note (i.e. date reminder):_____

_____

_____

Website:_____

Username:_____

Password:_____

Last 3 Passwords:_____

Important to Note (i.e. date reminder):_____

_____

》《·》《·》《·》《·》《·》《·》《·》《·》《·

_____

Website:_____

Username:_____

Password:_____

Last 3 Passwords:_____

Important to Note (i.e. date reminder):_____

_____

》《·》《·》《·》《·》《·》《·》《·》《·》《·

_____

Website:_____

Username:_____

Password:_____

Last 3 Passwords:_____

Important to Note (i.e. date reminder):_____

_____

_____

Website:_____

Username:_____

Password:_____

Last 3 Passwords:_____

Important to Note (i.e. date reminder):_____

_____

》《·》《·》《·》《·》《·》《·》《·》《·》《·

_____

Website:_____

Username:_____

Password:_____

Last 3 Passwords:_____

Important to Note (i.e. date reminder):_____

_____

》《·》《·》《·》《·》《·》《·》《·》《·》《·

_____

Website:_____

Username:_____

Password:_____

Last 3 Passwords:_____

Important to Note (i.e. date reminder):_____

_____

_____

Website:_____

Username:_____

Password:_____

Last 3 Passwords:_____

Important to Note (i.e. date reminder):_____

_____

》《·》《·》《·》《·》《·》《·》《·》《·》《·》《·

_____

Website:_____

Username:_____

Password:_____

Last 3 Passwords:_____

Important to Note (i.e. date reminder):_____

_____

》《·》《·》《·》《·》《·》《·》《·》《·》《·》《·

_____

Website:_____

Username:_____

Password:_____

Last 3 Passwords:_____

Important to Note (i.e. date reminder):_____

_____

_____

Website:_____

Username:_____

Password:_____

Last 3 Passwords:_____

Important to Note (i.e. date reminder):_____

_____

»《·》《·》《·》《·》《·》《·》《·》《·》《·》《·

_____

Website:_____

Username:_____

Password:_____

Last 3 Passwords:_____

Important to Note (i.e. date reminder):_____

_____

»《·》《·》《·》《·》《·》《·》《·》《·》《·》《·

_____

Website:_____

Username:_____

Password:_____

Last 3 Passwords:_____

Important to Note (i.e. date reminder):_____

_____

_____

Website:_____

Username:_____

Password:_____

Last 3 Passwords:_____

Important to Note (i.e. date reminder):_____

_____

≫《•≫《•≫《•≫《•≫《•≫《•≫《•≫《•≫《•≫《•

_____

Website:_____

Username:_____

Password:_____

Last 3 Passwords:_____

Important to Note (i.e. date reminder):_____

_____

≫《•≫《•≫《•≫《•≫《•≫《•≫《•≫《•≫《•

_____

Website:_____

Username:_____

Password:_____

Last 3 Passwords:_____

Important to Note (i.e. date reminder):_____

_____

USERNAMES & PASSWORDS THAT HAVE BEEN BURNED

Website:_____

Username:_____

Password:_____

Last 3 Passwords:_____

Important to Note (i.e. date reminder):_____

_____

Website:_____

Username:_____

Password:_____

Last 3 Passwords:_____

Important to Note (i.e. date reminder):_____

_____

Website:_____

Username:_____

Password:_____

Last 3 Passwords:_____

Important to Note (i.e. date reminder):_____

_____

USERNAMES & PASSWORDS THAT HAVE BEEN BURNED

Website:_____

Username:_____

Password:_____

Last 3 Passwords:_____

Important to Note (i.e. date reminder):_____

_____

Website:_____

Username:_____

Password:_____

Last 3 Passwords:_____

Important to Note (i.e. date reminder):_____

_____

Website:_____

Username:_____

Password:_____

Last 3 Passwords:_____

Important to Note (i.e. date reminder):_____

_____

USERNAMES & PASSWORDS THAT HAVE BEEN BURNED

Website:_____

Username:_____

Password:_____

Last 3 Passwords:_____

Important to Note (i.e. date reminder):_____

_____

Website:_____

Username:_____

Password:_____

Last 3 Passwords:_____

Important to Note (i.e. date reminder):_____

_____

Website:_____

Username:_____

Password:_____

Last 3 Passwords:_____

Important to Note (i.e. date reminder):_____

_____

USERNAMES & PASSWORDS THAT HAVE BEEN BURNED

Website:_____

Username:_____

Password:_____

Last 3 Passwords:_____

Important to Note (i.e. date reminder):_____

_____

Website:_____

Username:_____

Password:_____

Last 3 Passwords:_____

Important to Note (i.e. date reminder):_____

_____

Website:_____

Username:_____

Password:_____

Last 3 Passwords:_____

Important to Note (i.e. date reminder):_____

_____

Made in the USA
Las Vegas, NV
19 March 2021